Snap books®

costume
PARTIES

Planning a *Party* that Makes
Your Friends Say "*Wow!*"

by Jen Jones

CAPSTONE PRESS
a capstone imprint

Snap Books are published by Capstone Press,
1710 Roe Crest Drive, North Mankato, Minnesota 56003
www.capstonepub.com

Library of Congress Cataloging-in-Publication Data
Jones, Jen.
  Costume parties : planning a party that makes your friends say "wow!" / by Jen Jones.
      pages cm. — (Snap books. Perfect parties.)
  Summary: "Learn how to throw a costume party that will go down in history. Discover themes, decorations, food, and planning tips that will kick off the perfect party"— Provided by publisher.
  ISBN 978-1-4765-4007-8 (library binding)
  ISBN 978-1-4765-6054-0 (eBook PDF)
1. Children's parties—Planning—Juvenile literature. 2. Costume—Juvenile literature. I. Title.

  GV1205.J643 2014
  793.21--dc23   2013043385

Editorial Credits
Mari Bolte, editor; Tracy Davies McCabe, designer; Kathy McColley, production specialist;
Sarah Schuette, photo stylist; Sarah Schuette and Marcy Morin, project creators

Photo Credits
Photography by Capstone Studio: Karon Dubke except: Dreamstime: Dmitriy Shironosov, 24 (top), Shutterstock: Alliance, 12, Andrew Burgess, 8 (bottom), BooHoo, 11 (bottom), chrisbrignell, 24 (bottom), dgmata, 7 (middle), Edyta Pawlowska, 23 (front), Elena Elisseeva, 9, Firman Wahyudin, 29, Jackiso, 8 (top), Kalenik Hanna, 31, kearia, 10 (right), LanKS, 7 (top), Lena Pantiukh, 11 (top), nikkytok, 24 (left), Ozgur Coskun, 7 (bottom), pink pig, 11 (right, back), Ruth Black, 6, Sarah Cates, 18, sittipong, 10 (left), Susan McKenzie, 15 (top right) Tatiana Popova, 20, Teeratas, 17 (bottom), Vasya Kobelev, 11 (left), VolkOFF-ZS-BP, cover (middle), 16 (top)

Design Elements:
Shutterstock: Andrey_Kuzmin, Adrei Zarubaika, Cecilia Lim H M, Garsya, More Images, nikkytok, Petrosg, Yganko

Printed in the United States of America in Brainerd, Minnesota.
092013   007770BANGS14

TABLE OF CONTENTS

Getting Started **4**

The Big Idea **6**

Get in Check **8**

Party Pals **10**

Do the Math **12**

A Pirate P-arrrrrty **14**

Party Like A Rock Star **16**

Hot Rods **18**

Crepe Expectations **20**

Insta-Atmosphere: Quick Tricks **22**

Karaoke Queens **24**

Amazeballs **26**

It's Over! Now What? **28**

Gracias, Merci, Thank You! **30**

Read More **32**

Internet Sites **32**

Getting Started

It's not hard to see why people love parties so much. After all, they're festive, fun, and celebrate something that's really important—friendship. The best hostesses throw parties that bring new people together. That's where you come in!

The trick is planning a party that your friends won't forget. Creativity is the key—any interest or hobby can be transformed into a party theme. Get inspired with two unforgettable party ideas. A Pirate P-arrrrrty will have your friends saying, "Aye!" to more get-togethers. Party Like A Rock Star will help your guests find their inner divas. First, pick your theme. Then find oodles of ideas for making your party pop!

Of course, it's true that a hostess' work is never done. Endless to-do lists and lots of hands-on tasks often translate to lots of hard work for a hostess. Luckily, it can be a lot of fun—and a lot easier with the right insider intel! The right info can keep you organized, savvy, and sane as you plan your big shindig. Learn ways to cover all of the bases while preparing for your party—and hit a home run with the result.

The Big Idea

There's always a reason to celebrate! But sometimes the best parties are for no reason at all. Throwing a costume party is a great way to show your creativity. It also gives you a reason to gather your BFFs just for the fun of it. Using themes and costumes adds an extra layer of fun. It also gives your guests an idea of what to expect at the event.

Where can you find a killer theme idea? Let us count the ways! There are lots of resources to help spark a lightbulb moment. Choose one of the themes in this book, or search the Web for more ideas! Party-planning sites have whole sections devoted to different themes, color palettes, and designs. From darling décor to super sips, you'll find no shortage of inspiration!

Otaku Party

Turn up the J-pop and greet your guests with "kon'nichiwa!" Send out origami or mini manga invites. Challenge attendees to dress in Harajuku style, or dare them to show up in their cutest kigurumi. Serve bento boxes while watching everyone's favorite anime flicks. Decorate cupcakes with frosted cherry blossoms, or top them with round, red sprinkles to represent the Japanese flag. Send guests home with a pair of their own chopsticks.

Bookworm Bash

Choose your favorite popular series to celebrate. Have everyone bring a copy of their favorite book to compare, or host a trivia contest. Ask guests to dress as their favorite character. Serve food mentioned in the book. Make rolls or mockingjay cookies for a Hunger Games party. Find pumpkin juice, onion soup, or treacle tart recipes to celebrate Harry Potter. Hand out book covers or bookmarks for favors. Then ask your friends for suggestions for your next bookworm bash!

Murder Mystery

Whodunnit? Put on your sassiest detective hat and invite friends over for a night of intrigue. As far as party prep, buying a themed murder mystery kit is your best bet. Most kits include everything from the storyline to character descriptions to props!

Morning Mania

Don't want to wait for the party to start? Get everyone moving by hosting a morning party! Serve pancake pops and freshly squeezed orange juice, or set up a donut decorating bar. Have guests show up in their jammies. (Tell them to bring sleeping bags for breakfast "in bed!")

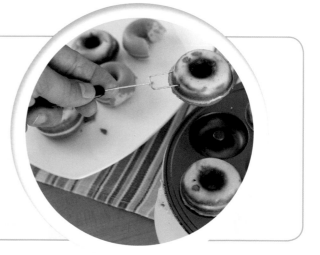

Get in Check

Use this page as a one-stop shop for all things party prep! This general checklist covers all of the to-do's that need to happen before your shindig.

4 to 6 Weeks Ahead

☐ get your parents' permission

☐ finalize the details—date, theme, location, etc.

☐ research costs and set a budget

☐ make your guest list

☐ rent any needed equipment (such as a karaoke machine)

☐ start getting jazzed for your party!

3 Weeks Ahead

☐ assemble and send out invites

☐ start planning the menu and signature sips

☐ make a list of necessary supplies and décor

2 Weeks Ahead

 figure out the fun stuff—games, music, favors

 shop for non-perishable items like favors and décor

1 Week Ahead

 collect all RSVPs and finalize guest count

 assemble any gift bags/décor

make your party playlists

1 to 3 Days Ahead

 buy food and drink items, as well as any other necessities not already purchased

prepare as much food as possible and store in the refrigerator or freezer

clean the house and/or backyard

Party Pals

Curious what "R.S.V.P." stands for? Wonder no more. It stems from the French phrase *Répondez, s'il vous plait*. In other words, "Please reply!"

R.S.V.P.s are great tools for hostesses. Most event planning experts say to expect anywhere from one-half to two-thirds of your invited guests to show up. Even with that stat, it's nice to have a concrete number! Requesting an R.S.V.P. provides just that by helping you keep track of who is—and isn't—able to make it to your party.

When sending invites, be sure to include a deadline to respond. The deadline date should be at least one week before the party date. If you don't hear back from everyone in time, just make a casual phone call or e-mail to follow up. Once you have a final list, you'll know who your party peeps are!

Ask Mizz Manners

Q. DO I HAVE TO INVITE EVERYONE IN MY CLASS?

A. Always a tricky question! It's a nice gesture to invite as many people as possible. But sometimes budget, location, or other factors just won't allow it. The best thing to do in this situation is to avoid hurt feelings.

Avoid passing out invites at school. Instead, e-mail or send invites directly to your friends' homes. If anyone asks why he or she wasn't invited, just be honest. Simply say that this time you're keeping it small, but you'd love to host a bigger bash in the future! (More excuses for parties? Yes, please.)

Do the Math

Before you can start planning, setting a budget is a must! Start by setting an overall spending limit. Talk with your parents about what they are willing to contribute to the party. Add that to the amount you've planned to spend. (For example, if you're contributing $50 and your parents are giving $100, you've got $150 to work with.) Divide that total by the number of people expected to attend. That's how much you can spend per person.

Next, figure out what's most important to you. Is it décor? Entertainment? Food and beverages? Making a list of priorities will help you see how to divide the funds. As you shop, keep a running expense total so that you don't blow the budget!

The Look for Less

Don't stress if you're not on a Beverly Hills budget. It's more than possible to throw a memorable party that feels—and looks—like a million bucks. Believe it or not, the dollar store can be a source of lots of super-cute, useful finds. Look there for anything from colorful drinking glasses to art supplies. It's a fun place to go on a supermarket sweep!

Quick Swaps For Saving Moolah

snail mail invites	⟫⟫➤	e-mail
super-sized guest list	⟫⟫➤	smaller guest list
full menu	⟫⟫➤	apps and desserts
paper plates and cups	⟫⟫➤	plates and cups your family owns

PARTY BUDGET

Party Budget Total: _____

Item	% of Budget	$ Allowance	$ Parents
FOOD	50%		
DECORATIONS	25%		
INVITATIONS	10%		
TABLEWARE	5%		
FAVORS	5%		
MISC.	5%		

PARTY LIKE A ROCK STAR

Pump up the volume and take center stage with this rockin' party theme.

THE LOOK

To party like a star, you have to look the part. Ask your guests to dress like their favorite pop princess. Or challenge them to design their own diva look! Neon clip-on hair extensions, ripped jeans, and crazy prints are all fair game.

In-Style Invite

Who wouldn't love an all-access pass to your VIP bash? Spread the word with style. Hand out laminated backstage pass-style invites clipped on glittery lanyards.

Get Inked Here
⇓

Setting the Stage

Set up a mock tattoo parlor filled with bold body art stickers. Your friends will love comparing their temporary ink.

Paparazzi alert! Set up a table full of fun props such as boas, sunglasses, and inflatable guitars. Hang a sheet as a photo backdrop. Then ask a camera-savvy relative to take some shots of your friends posing. Or snap them with a cell phone to share them in an instant.

Eats and Treats

Live out loud with these killer microphone cupcakes!

- dark frosting
- colored cake cones
- baked cupcakes
- dark sugar sprinkles

Spread a thin layer of frosting inside the upper part of the cake cone. (This will help hold the cupcake in place.) Place the cupcake inside the cone, bottom-side-down. Frost the top of the cupcake. Roll the frosted cupcake in sprinkles.

*Tip: An ice cream cone cupcake baking rack will make frosting easier. If you can't find one, cut cone-sized holes in the bottom of a disposable roasting pan or cereal box. Then flip the pan upside down before setting a cupcake cone in each hole.

YOU'VE GOT GAME

Crank things up a notch by holding a battle of the air bands! Challenge your fellow rockers to show off their air guitar skills. You can even stage a tournament. Have your friends face off to see who's got star quality to spare. Try karaoke or band video games for another off-the-charts option.

Signature Sip: The Rock-Tail

This mocktail is destined to be a #1 hit!

- 4 tablespoons (60 milliliters) grenadine
- 16 ounces (.47 liters) ginger ale
- Pop Rocks
- lollipop

Mix grenadine with ginger ale. Serve in a martini glass rimmed with Pop Rocks. Garnish each glass with a lollipop.

Favors with Flair:

- neon plastic sunglasses
- custom playlist suggestions

Hot Rods

A good hostess never gets salty-unless she's prepping pretzels! Dipped pretzel rods are an easy and fun way to impress your guests. From chocolate to caramel, there are plenty of sugary coatings to pair with pretzels.

Chocolate Dippers

1 cup (240 mL) chocolate chips
1 tablespoon (15 mL) vegetable oil

Caramel Coated

½ pound (255 grams) soft caramels
2 tablespoons (30 mL) cream

Instructions for both:

1. Place ingredients in a microwave-safe bowl and heat for 30 seconds. Remove bowl and stir. Repeat until coating is completely melted and smooth.

2. Dip a pretzel rod into the coating, leaving the last third of the pretzel uncovered.

3. While the coating is still wet, roll pretzel in topping of your choice. For extra flair, drizzle colored candy melts over topped pretzel rods.

GO BEYOND NUTS AND SPRINKLES! FOR GOURMET COMBOS, TRY:

- white chocolate chips and chopped dried cranberries

- peanuts, mini marshmallows, and mini chocolate chips

- shredded coconut, crushed banana chips, and almonds

- a layer of caramel, a layer of chocolate, and chopped pecans

Get Crafty

Make your pretzels part of your party theme!
Coat them with silver sugar to make pirate swords.
Use black sugar for cannons.

Use a small piping bag to decorate each pretzel rod with tiny mustaches.

Use melted chocolate to attach a pretzel ring to the end of each rod to make a monocle.

Crepe Expectations

Add a touch of insta-glam with a shower of streamers. This colorful crepe paper chandelier is a simple yet stylish project. It's sure to make your party décor pop.

All the Essentials:

- measuring tape
- crepe paper in different colors
- hole punch
- double-sided tape
- 1 12-inch (30.5 cm) embroidery hoop
- ribbon or twine

1. Decide where to hang your chandelier. Use a measuring tape to decide how long the streamers should be. Once you have settled on a length, cut a streamer twice your measurement.

2. Measure and cut enough streamers to cover half the hoop.

3. Punch a line of circles along the edges of the crepe paper. The holes should be about an inch (2.5 cm) apart.

4. Stick a piece of double-sided tape around the inside of the embroidery hoop. Wrap the top part of a streamer around it so that it sticks to the tape.

5. Tape the end of the streamer to the opposite side of the embroidery hoop.

6. Repeat steps 4 and 5 until you've worked your way around the hoop. Use as many streamers as you like until you have the look you want.

7. Cut three pieces of ribbon or twine to 18-inch (46 cm) lengths. Evenly space each ribbon around the hoop. Tie the ribbon to the hoop, in between the streamers.

8. Knot the three ribbons together in the center of the hoop. Use them to hang the chandelier.

Adding Drama

Why stop at one? Use 8-inch (20 cm) embroidery hoops to make two smaller chandeliers. Hang one on either side of the larger chandelier.

Use self-adhesive gemstones to give the chandelier some extra glitz.

To make these pirate-themed, use black, red, and white streamers.

Insta-Atmosphere: Quick Tricks

Create a DIY table runner using pretty wrapping paper. Layer two or more colors or patterns for more depth. Scatter vase gems or flat glass marbles over the top for some glittery color.

Printables add polish to your display and décor. They also give your guests a heads up on where to sit and what's on the menu! Use signs and labels to set off your spread.

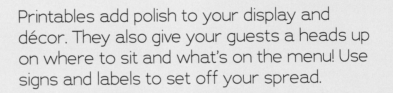

Play with lighting to provide an instant room makeover. Switch out regular lightbulbs for ones with color, or simply dim the lights to add a bit of mood lighting. String lights are also a quick fix for soft lighting.

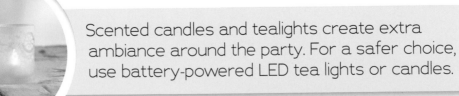

Scented candles and tealights create extra ambiance around the party. For a safer choice, use battery-powered LED tea lights or candles.

A balloon wall will make your party pop! Tape balloons of all different colors and designs on a big wall. String balloons onto a banner and write giant letters on them to spell out your theme. Fill white balloons with colored confetti or bits of tissue paper before blowing them up. Or go extra-large with huge round balloons!

Karaoke Queens

Setting up a karaoke station will get all of your guests in (lip) sync. Let everyone release their rock star side with these ideas for simple karaoke setup.

- Download a karaoke app for instant access to tunes. All you have to do is plug your phone into the TV and start singing.

- If you want to really rock the mic, buy a microphone! Some microphones plug right into your music player. You can sing songs from your own music library or the mic's collection. Others let you record performances so that your party guests can remember their rock star moment after the party ends.

- Don't forget to make your karaoke "club" feel funky! Add a zebra-striped rug or lay a piano keyboard-style runner under the TV. Hang zig-zag accordion streamers from the ceiling as a backdrop. Disco or strobe lights will also help set the stage for your friends to take the spotlight.

Song Selection

Be prepared for guests to call dibs on "their" song. If two of your guests pick the same solo, suggest they sing it together.

For maximum crowd participation, pick songs that everyone can sing along to!

Keep the songs on the shorter side. Songs with long openings or instrumental breaks can bring the room's energy down. Four minutes or less is a good starting point.

Unless you're a karaoke pro, avoid rap or songs that use Autotune.

Share and Share Alike

Rule number one: Don't hog the mic! Make sure everyone who wants to sing takes a turn. An easy way to avoid a stage hog is to set rules before the party starts. For example, everyone has to sing at least once before someone gets to go again. Or have guests draw numbers so everyone has to wait their turn.

Extra Applause!

Karaoke is about having fun! Self-conscious guests may feel nervous about singing in front of a crowd. Help them feel at ease by having familiar tunes available, or offering to be their backup. Get your audience on board, too! A pumped-up crowd will help even the shyest singer open up.

On that note, don't force a timid singer to take a turn. If they want to sing, they'll put in their own song request.

Take a number! Have karaoke request slips available so your friends can get their faves on the list.

SONG SLIP

NAME:

SONG:

Amazeballs

Impress your friends with this quick, easy, and delicious cookie buttery treat!

- two bananas, mashed
- 1 cup (240 mL) quick oats
- ¼ cup (60 mL) chocolate candies
- 2 tablespoons (30 mL) cookie butter (also called speculoos or biscoff spread)
- 1 teaspoon (5 mL) vanilla extract
- nonstick baking sheet
- 1 cup (240 mL) white chocolate chips

1. Preheat the oven to 350°F (180°C).
3. Mix bananas, oats, candies, cookie butter, and vanilla together.
3. Take a spoonful of the mixture and roll it into a ball. Place the balls a few inches apart on a nonstick baking sheet.
4. Bake the cookies inside the oven for 15 minutes. Remove hot tray with oven mitts.
5. Drizzle melted white chocolate over cooled cookies.

Ask Mizz Manners

Q. WHAT FOODS SHOULD A HOSTESS AVOID SERVING?

A. Different experts will give different answers, but certain foods are widely thought to be party "don'ts." If you can, steer clear of messy finger foods like Buffalo wings and cheesy chips. They may be finger-lickin' good, but sticky or orange fingers are no fun. Also avoid stinky cheeses, fish dishes, anything garlicky, and hard-boiled eggs. Your nose will thank you.

Q. HELP! HOW MUCH FOOD IS TOO MUCH?

A. When it comes to party planning, always round up! Expect people to eat more than you think. Anticipate more guests arriving than you planned for. It's better to have too much than too little. Also, try to figure out which items might be the most popular. Bulk up on the foods that have a higher chance of being scarfed first.

If you can't buy any more of a main dish, have snacks such as nuts, veggies, or chips on hand. Snacks will help your guests fill up without stressing out your wallet.

Q: I'M ON A BUDGET. HOW CAN I FEED MY GUESTS ON A LIMITED AMOUNT OF MOOLAH?

A. Just because cash is tight doesn't mean you can't host a delicious get-together. Keep things low-key by holding a movie night with a popcorn bar. Host a tea or cocktail party and serve just appetizers or desserts. Quiches, pasta salads, and chilis are easy, cost-effective, and serve a crowd. For something more rustic, get outdoors! Roast hot dogs, baked potatoes, and marshmallows. There are tons of meal ideas for the hostess with limited funds!

It's Over! Now What?

The party's over! Wishing you could fast forward to the part where the house is clean again? Though you can't wave a magic wand, there are plenty of ways to get your space spic-and-span in a snap.

- [ ] Form a cleanup crew. See if you can bribe your sibs or a few friends to stay afterward and keep the party going. You can entertain yourselves by dishing the "dirt" from the party.

- [ ] Check for any carpet or furniture stains. If you happen to find one, soak it up with a paper towel, then apply stain remover according to the directions (or your parents!)

- [ ] Do a clean sweep of the party area. Use two trash bags to separate actual trash and recyclable items.

- [ ] Place all usable leftover food in containers, and dispose of the rest. Keep in mind how long each food item has been at room temperature, and how well it will keep.

- [ ] Load the dishwasher and let it run as you clean. No dishwasher? No problem. Let dishes soak in the sink as you clean.

- [ ] For an indoor party, vacuum and/or mop floors in the areas where your guests hung out.

- [ ] Store any pieces of décor, party favors, or other items you want to save in a large plastic bin. You can also hang a few pieces in your room as a memento of your mega-awesome day.

Tips on Speeding Up The Clean Up Before, During, and After

Start the party with the cleanest possible space. Your house will be back to spic-and-span with just a quick wipe-down after the party.

Use disposable cups, plates, and other servingware to minimize dish washing time. If you're concerned about waste, look into compostable or biodegradable items.

Have plenty of trash cans available during the party. Label any non-trash cans, such as recyclables or compostables. Your guests will clean up after themselves.

Send your guests home with leftovers. You'll spend less time looking for fridge space after the party.

Gracias, Merci, Thank You!

The good news: the party was a smash success. The bad news: it's true that a hostess' job is never done! Even if your party didn't involve gifts, thanking guests just for being there is the classy thing to do. Luckily, the secrets to writing thank-you notes are simple.

Always send within two weeks of the party date. Set time aside after the party for this task so you don't forget. Buy nice stationary, stamps, and a great pen before the party. It won't seem like such a chore if you're looking forward to it!

Read More

Bolte, Mari. *Harajuku Style: Fun Fashions You Can Sketch.* Drawing Fun Fashions. North Mankato, Minn.: Capstone Press, 2013.

Martini, Angela. *A Smart Girl's Guide to Parties: How to be a Great Guest, Be a Happy Hostess, and Have Fun at Any Kind of Party.* Be Your Best. Middleton, Wisc.: American Girl, 2010.

Turnbull, Stephanie. *Cards and Gifts: Style Secrets for Girls.* Girl Talk. Mankato, Minn.: Smart Apple Media, 2014.

Internet Sites

FactHound offers a safe, fun way to find Internet sites related to this book. All of the sites on FactHound have been researched by our staff.

Here's all you do:

Visit *www.facthound.com*

Type in this code: 9781476540078

 Check out projects, games and lots more at
www.capstonekids.com